T0064249

WHEN 40 ACRES AND A MULE WON'T DO!

Retirement is Not an Age, But a Financial Number

LASHAUNDRA CAESAR

WESTBOW
PRESS®
A DIVISION OF THOMAS NELSON
& ZONDERVAN

WestBow Press books may be ordered through booksellers or by contacting:

WestBow Press
A Division of Thomas Nelson & Zondervan
1663 Liberty Drive
Bloomington, IN 47403
www.westbowpress.com
844-714-3454

Scripture taken from the King James Version of the Bible.

ISBN: 978-1-6642-1982-3 (sc)
ISBN: 978-1-6642-1983-0 (hc)
ISBN: 978-1-6642-1984-7 (e)

Library of Congress Control Number: 2021901588

Print information available on the last page.

WestBow Press rev. date: 03/12/2021

ACKNOWLEDGEMENTS

I am so thankful for the love of God in my life. He is the author and finisher of my faith. I am grateful to my parents Bill and Janie Caesar, who are resting in heaven for making sure they taught me about God, forgiveness and instilled in me a "work hard" mentality. My mother was very creative in designing African attire and taking pictures of every event in my hometown of Kingsville, Texas. This is where I developed the entrepreneurship spirit. My father Chief Joe Bill Caesar served his country for over twenty-six years in the United States Navy. He taught me how to be a strong independent woman. Dad also showed me how to save and handle money. He loved to cook, build anything of wood and go camping. Dad was a collector of coins. I am truly grateful for loving parents who loved God and I thank God for blessing me with these loving parents.

The writing of this book "When 40 Acres and a Mule Won't Do" has been a book in my heart and soul for over six years. I would like to thank a few people who helped to bring this book into the forefront for change. First, I would like to thank my wife Mary Hall Caesar who encouraged me to put my passion onto paper. She was my inspiration and motivation to keep things flowing while I spent countless hours writing. Mary was also my first editor. An author friend of mine named Geraldine Guadagno was very helpful in sharing some writing pointers with me and giving me some useful tips in publishing my book. A big thank you to John and Sharon Konvicka, who explained to me the value in investing my hard-earned money when I was twenty-seven years old instead of buying depreciation goods. I would like to thank all of my clients, friends, family, church family and participants who attended my financial workshops and boot camps over the years. Thank you all for your prayers and support of this endeavor. I can't forget to mention my childhood Pastor Rev. Earl Jackson of King Star Baptist Church who encouraged me to become a speaker and let my voice be heard to inspire others to succeed. My current Pastor Rev. Dr. William H. Knight was very supportive in encouraging me to continue making a difference in the world. Through his words, deeds and prayers he was always providing support and encouraging my journey. Finally, I would like to thank the members of my publishing and editing team from WestBow Press a division of Thomas Nelson.

May everyone who read, touch and share this book with others in this world be blessed beyond measure. Remember knowledge is power but application is success!

ABOUT THE AUTHOR

LaShaundra Caesar was born and raised in Kingsville, Texas. There she graduated from H.M. King High School and Texas A & I University with a degree in elementary education. She earned her Masters' Degree and Administrative Certification from University of Texas San Antonio. She played basketball in high school and college. LaShaundra knew she wanted to be a teacher and a high school varsity basketball coach. Her education and desire to coach led her to San Antonio where in 1997 her basketball team "The Lady Hornets" from East Central H.S. went to the state basketball tournament. She taught and coached for over thirty-two years. The last eight years were spent as an assistant principal and a vice principal in both public

and private schools. With the true heart and love of coaching and motivating she became a certified financial life coach through the National Financial Literacy Educator's Council and Dave Ramsey's Master Coaching Courses. After becoming a certified financial life coach, she went on her own financial literacy campaign. She opened an office under "Caesar-Time" Financial Life Coach LLC, as chief executive officer and she then expanded her services to offer pension reviews, mortgage protection, living benefits and final expenses to her clients. She makes her home in San Antonio, Texas with her wife and their two dogs. She will be more than happy to answer any questions you may have at the following website: caesarsfinancialgroup.com

PREFACE

Financial illiteracy has reached epidemic proportions in our country and causes major problems at both the community and national levels. Eight out of ten people in America are living paycheck to paycheck which contributes to sleepless nights, stress, illnesses and hopelessness. Sadly, some people turn to suicide as their way out of the bondage of debt. "When 40 Acres and a Mule Won't Do" was written to offer solutions to addressing these issues. We will glance back at what did and did not happen back in the year 1865 with Special Field Orders 15, then move forward into what we can change to create a debt free/wealth building America for all people.

Our schools, until recently did not teach financial literacy, so we have missed the boat in that aspect. We were probably taught the basics such as reading, writing and math and some homemaking, art and physical education. Even in college, we were taught the skills needed to get a job, but never how to manage our money and save for the future. "When 40 Acres and a Mule Won't Do" gets to the heart of the problem. This book is straight to the point with easy to understand text and strategies to read and apply to your financial situations. Know that most of us have made mistakes with money. This is normal, especially in our younger years, but as we reach our late twenties and early thirties life begins to send us a few challenges like: purchasing a home, saving for college for our children and paying off those student loans. Another challenge could be finding that one career we can be happy with for the next thirty to forty years. We may be able to retire sooner, if we know how money really works and start to apply these strategies as soon as possible. Some of these tips and strategies can be implemented in 10 minutes or less.

HOW TO BEST READ AND STUDY THIS BOOK

Look at the key words which will be included in the chapter

Read the section (you may want to have a bible close by to reference some scriptures)

Write down in the spaces provided anything you want to remember

Read the discussion questions and answer them

Now read the activities for the section. I encourage you to talk these over with a significate other or your spouse, if you have one.

CONTENTS

Introduction...xvii

Chapter 1   Financial Psychology and our Mindset 1
    Acre #1 – Snapshot of America in 2020 2
    Acre #2 – Easy on the Dopamine... 2
    Acre #3 – The Monthly Cycle of Money 3

Chapter 2   Budgeting Your Money and Getting Out of Debt............ 5
    Acre #4 – Building a Healthy Relationship with Money 5
    Acre #5 – What Do Wealthy, Middle and Low Income
    People Buy?... 6
    Acre #6 – Setting a Budget for your Family that Works................. 8
    Acre #7 – Steps in Paying Cash with the Envelope Method 10
    Acre #8 – Good News About Debt... 12

Chapter 3   Biblical Plans for our Finances and Giving Back............15
    Acre #9 – Have Our Priorities In Order... 16
    Acre #10 – Why Does A Good Steward Give Back 17

Chapter 4   Credit Profile 21
    Acre #11 – Debt is the Wealth Killer.. 22
    Acre #12 – Know the Differences in Good and Bad Credit.......... 23
    Acre #13 – What is the Range of Credit Scores?........................... 23
    Acre #14 – How to Improve My Credit Scores.............................. 24

Chapter 5   How to Buy A Vehicle and Save Thousands 27
    Acre #15 – Know How to Negotiate your Next Vehicle Deal 28

Chapter 6   Taxes and Allowances 33
    Acre #16 – Property Taxes 34
    Acre #17 – What about Income Taxes? 34
    Acre #18 – Want a raise, then give yourself one! 34
    Acre #19 – Factors to Be Considered When Filling Out Your
    W-4 Withholdings 36
    Acre #20 – Stay Home and Build Your Own Business! 37

Chapter 7   Insurance and Estate Planning 41
    Acre #21 – Woo-Who .... Let's Talk About Insurance 42
    Acre #22 – Compare the Basic Two Types of Life Insurance 43
    Acre #23 – New Development in Life Insurance, Mortgage
    Protection, and Final Expenses 45
    Acre #24 – What Other Types of Insurance are Necessary? 46
    Acre #25 – Estate Planning is Vital for Everyone 47

Chapter 8   Interest and "The Rule of 72" 51
    Acre #26 – Knowing this Rule can Make or Break You 52

Chapter 9   Making Student Loans Affordable 55
    Acre #27 – Be Smart About College Cost 56
    Acre #28 – Never Stop Learning 58

Chapter 10   Retirement Plan and Business Savvy 61
    Acre #29 – What to Consider Before Retiring? 61
    Acre #30 – Retirement is not an Age but a Financial Number! 64
    Acre #31 – You Want to Start Your Own Business and be
    Your Own Boss? 64
    Acre #32 – The Important Business Plan 67

Chapter 11   Investing 101 73
    Acre #33 – Risks and Growth in Balance 74
    Acre #34 – Compound Interest Builds Wealth 74

Chapter 12   Investments in Real Estate 79

    Acre #35 – There are Only a Few Things You Can Do With

    Money 80

    Acre #36 – Ways to Create Wealth in Real Estate 81

    Acre #37 – Which Type of Real Estate Deals are Best for You? 82

    Acre #38 – Example of a Buy and Hold Deal 82

    Acre #39 – Make a Whopping 25 – 50% Interest in Texas 83

    Acre #40 – "The Big Ideas" 84

Chapter 13   The Mule 87

INTRODUCTION

America, the land of the free and the home of the brave, but freedom has a price. In this book "When 40 Acres and a Mule Won't Do" I want to look at the events that did and did not happen and what we as a people and eighty percent of all Americans need to know about money and finances. How can we bring debt down and build wealth up for our families amid uncertainty for the year 2021 and beyond?

Let us take a glance back to when the Civil War was ending. At that time, the Union leaders held a meeting with a group of black ministers in Savannah, Georgia, the purpose of this meeting was to find out what the freed slaves wanted in order to bring financial stability to their families. After four days of discussions, General William T. Sherman came up with the Special Field Order 15. The order was to set aside land for the freed slaves along the coast from Charleston, S.C. to the St. Johns River in Florida. The mules were left over from the Army and were not in the agreement. General Sherman appointed Brig. General Rufus Saxton the duty of dividing up the land and giving up to forty acres of land to each family. The spokesmen for the black leaders was Rev. Garrison Frazier. When asked what the freed slaves wanted, he replied, "We want to be free from the domination of white men, we want to be educated and have our own land."

Dr. Stan Deaton from the Georgia Historical Society stated after President Abraham Lincoln was assassinated, his successor, President Andrew Johnson reversed Sherman's Special Field Order 15, giving all of the land back to the former confederate owners. This act of reversal on the Special Order 15 had a historical effect on the economic wealth and stability of the freed slaves and their families for generations to come. The freed slaves had few options of providing for their families, much less building generational wealth. Just thinking and wondering.....Where would African American families be today in the year 2021, if we had been given the forty acres?

As I stated, we can glance back, but let's focus forward. The forty acres and a mule never happened 156 years ago for the freed slave. Today this would be worth over $6.4 trillion dollars (Yes! Journal-Tracy Loeffelholz Dunnjeff Neumann May 14, 2015) With the advancements and benefits, we enjoy as Americans, has our focus to provide for our families to the best of our abilities been placed on the back burner? Have we lost focus on the difference between wants and needs? Has the ability to create real wealth been replaced with the media's portrayal of what wealth looks like? Wealth is not just looking the part. Are we as Americans driving cars way above our means? Are we buying designer clothes, purses and shoes we cannot afford? Is our paycheck at the mercy of our children's desire to have expensive technology, games and toys? Are we sitting and waiting on the latest version of a cell phone to hit the shelves? Do we save enough for long term needs like: college, having our own business and home? Are we prepared to retire when we want and travel when and where we desire? Have we built up generational wealth not only for our children, but our children's children? Our ancestor thought about their family's financial future by providing their children a legacy to flourish. We have access to education like no other generation. Granted our schools did not provide and teach us about finances in the real world of our everyday living, until around 2015. The educational system missed the boat on teaching financial literacy. Probably, if you are like me, we had classes in reading, writing, science, social studies and arithmetic, along with a little physical education, music, and art, but no personal finance. It seems high schools and colleges are educating the student to become gainfully employed, but what about how to handle the money that is made? The financial steps in this book will teach you how to manage your money while building wealth. Maybe not 6.4 trillion dollars, but if followed, surely a nice nest egg. I myself have made many mistakes with money. I would buy a car and trade it in every two or three years and be upside down on the trade-in. When I got a new car financed, I was still paying on the old car along with the new car. I surely wasn't thinking about the difference of wants and needs because

I thought everything I wanted was a need. This is what I call stinking thinking for sure!

This is an area we must bring to the forefront of change. We can't afford to allow another generation to miss out on this valuable information. Knowledge is power! Whoever has the knowledge, has the power. If you walk into a car dealership and do not have the knowledge of the vehicle you want to purchase, along with the options, types of financing, rebates, the average cost of what others have paid for the same vehicle and your recent credit scores you don't have the power, they do! Knowledge is only useful if you use it by applying it to something. Knowledge is power, but application is success! So why not shift the power to you and the people you love? As you gain knowledge in all financial matters, you will have the confidence to share and teach these strategies to your children and grandchildren.

Like many of us, we work forty hours or more for forty years, just to retire on forty percent of what we were used to earning. If we are lucky or blessed to live another forty years, we just might go broke. If you want to continue to work well into your senior years, it should be by choice and not by necessity. A good education may open the doors of opportunity, but that is not always the case. You may have to knock on a lot of doors. If you do go to college, there is a way to save money by attending a community college, stay in your city or state, and/or stay at home, if you can. Be nice to your parents, so they won't turn your room into a den or game room. Out-of-State colleges and universities tuition are generally two to three times more expensive than in-state.

<u>Two ways you can become a millionaire</u>

Method #1- Most people make over $1,000,000 (million) in their lifetime. If a person makes only $30,000 a year and works for forty years, they have made $1,200,000. The problem is how much have you saved? Did you overpay your taxes and get a refund each year instead of bringing home the extra money and investing ten to fifteen percent? More on this later!

Method #2 - Start investing your money. Did you know if you start investing a mere $100 a month at the age of twenty-one in a mutual fund getting a return of at least eight percent, you will have over $1,000,000 by the time you are sixty-five years old. It may not be fast, but it is steady. More about this later!

My story of money and the addiction

My first job was a teacher/coach in 1982. I made a whopping $13,500, when Texas elected Mark White as the Governor and he gave teachers a raise. Thank you, Governor White! Then I was making $18,000. I had arrived! I had no plans, except to purchase a Nissan 300 ZX with a "T" top (Silver Shadow was her name). I looked **good** in it......**big afro** and all! The next three cars I purchased were a Mercedes-Benz 6.9, Audi 6 and a Lexus 300. I loved cars, probably was even addicted to them. Truth be told, we all have some type of addiction whether its cars, clothes, shoes, books, lotto, gambling, smoking, drinking, eating or _____, or whatever floats your boat. Now, I wish all those car purchases were houses instead. I did buy my first home in 1985, since homeownership has a lot of taxes advantages, but we will talk more on this later.

Stop the flossing
and
make your paper, work for you!

CHAPTER 1

Financial Psychology and our Mindset

Key Words

Dopamine – Neurotransmitters in the brain that send signals to the other nerves in the body (feel good sensation).

Fixed Mindset – Having a feeling that you will never improve and that you are stuck.

Flossing – (slang) Living beyond your means to impress others.

Growth Mindset – Having a feeling that you can improve and make positive changes where needed.

Mindset – How you feel about yourself.

Needs – Things that are necessary for living: food, water, air, sleep, clothes and shelter.

Psychology – The scientific study of the mind and behavior.

Wants – Things we desire beyond our basic needs: latest electronics, designer clothes, expensive vehicle, jewelry etc.

If we could get past this "stinking thinking" we could really prosper as a nation.

Acre #1 – Snapshot of America in 2020

Nearly fifty percent of Americans live paycheck to paycheck

Fifty percent of elderly women living alone, make less than $10,000 a year

Nearly 66 percent of all Americans have less than $500 in their savings

Almost 45 percent do not have a savings account

Forty-two percent of women have no money in their savings

Thirty-seven percent of parents do not feel comfortable talking to their children about money

Only Sixty-nine percent of Americans are saving ten percent or less for retirement

(www.gobankingrates.com)

Acre #2 – Easy on the Dopamine

Listen up America! We are spending far too much money on depreciating goods. Things that have little value or hardly any value after it is purchased. You have worked too hard for your money to just buy stuff we have to first respect our money. As the old folks used to say, money do not grow on trees, you worked hard for it, value your money. Can we blame this type of spending on dopamine? Dopamine is the neurotransmitter in the brain that travels to other nerves in our bodies and it makes us feel good. You know how we felt when we were kids opening our Christmas gifts. Especially, when we already knew what was inside the boxes, just saying. We could not wait to play with our favorite toy. As adults we still get that same type of feeling, even when we are just looking at "something" we really want.

Wealthy People Think Differently

Middle Class	Wealthy
Good education	Invest in good financial education
Work for their money	Have their money work for them
Seek job security through work	Build a business or businesses
Save money at low interest rates	Invest money
Do not want to take risks	Take minor risk to wealthy

Acre #3 – *The Monthly Cycle of Money*

WOW! Just got paid! Let us go out to eat, party, and buy ourselves something we think we deserve. As a matter of fact, let us do this multiple times this week. Stinking thinking will have you spending your money on wants and more wants. The middle of the month comes, and you are still spending like you just got paid. Once the end of the month arrives you do not know if you have enough money to buy food, pay the electric bill, keep the water on, or put gas in your car so you end up taking drastic measures to obtain money such as selling your car, hocking your TV or your wedding ring. Stop it please! So now what do you do? Ask a relative or a friend for a loan, try to get a pay-day loan, cash advance, play the lotto, or just rack up another late payment that will be reported to the three credit bureaus. Maybe you have spiraled into a downward depression and want it all to just go away. Under this kind of stress what kind of spouse or parent have you become? Are you angry and feeling hopeless at your situation? I pray not! Your help is in reading this book and asking God to help you implement the tips and strategies for financial success now and in the future. Most of these strategies and useful steps can be implemented in ten to fifteen minutes.

Knowledge is Power but Application is Success!!!

Notes (Things to remember)

_____

_____

_____

_____

_____

_____

"The rich ruleth over the poor, and the borrower is servant to the lender."
Proverbs 22:7 –(KJV)

Discussion Questions

1. Looking again at the verse above, what would your life look like if you did not have any debt? What would you and your family be doing right now if you were debt free?
2. Getting out of debt will take a lot of work and discipline. Name two things you can do immediately to start getting out of debt.
3. How would you feel about getting rid of your credit cards?

Activities:

How many credit cards do you own? How many do you use?

What would it take for you to pay cash for everything, except your home?

Continue reading this book to the end.

CHAPTER 2

Budgeting Your Money and Getting Out of Debt

<u>**Key Words**</u>

Appreciating Goods - Items that go up in value over time.

Consequences - The results of something that happened earlier.

Deprecating Goods - Items that go down in value quickly.

Emergency Fund - Money that should be used only in the event of an emergency.

Emotional Purchase - Buying things to make ourselves feel better.

Finances - The conduct or transaction of money matters.

Gazelle Intensity - Being intentional, truly focused.

Immediate Gratification - Wanting it now, not willing to wait.

Non-Essential Goods - Not necessary things to buy.

Acre #4 – Building a Healthy Relationship with Money

Is the love of money the root to all evil or is how we use it the evil? Could it be considered that greed is the evil? As an educator for over thirty-two years, I am familiar with the writing and teaching of Carol DeWitt's "Growth Mindset". She describes our two types of thinking and feeling about our situations and even how teachers feel about the abilities of their students. If we expect little from our students, we will get little (fixed). If we challenge our students, they will generally rise to the challenge (growth).

The first mindset is fixed. In a fixed mindset we feel this is the life that has been given to us and that is the way it is always going to be. I cannot change, so why try to improve, or grow? This fixed mindset can keep one in a dead-end job or no job at all. I am going to always live paycheck to paycheck no matter what I try. There is nothing better for me.

The second mindset is growth. In the growth mindset, there is no limit in our thinking of where we can go and what we can accomplish. I am at this point today, but if I can do "A, B or C", then I will go to the next level. In finances these people are creating a better life for themselves and their families.

Acre #5 – What Do Wealthy, Middle and Low Income People Buy?

Wealthy People Spend their Money on: "Money Making Assets" (Real Estate, Businesses, Stocks...etc.). Wealthy people are wealthy because they have habits of spending and investing which creates more wealth. Their thought processes before any deal or purchase is "Will this create more money?" It's not so much about the initial cost of the purchase, but how much profit or growth can be made with that purchase? What will be my return on investment (ROI)?

Middle Class People Spend Their Money on: "Assets" (houses, cars, international traveling and high-end electronics) and "Stuff/Things". The middle class have assets that need to be paid off or is not making them any money. These assets still are considered a liability. A house is not an asset until it becomes rental property and is generating a profit. Oh....and cars do not appreciate in value, so they are really a liability. These are the "Stuff/Things" we like to buy. Do not try to keep up with the "JONES" since you do not live with them. They may be struggling to make ends meet and living paycheck to paycheck.

Low Income People Spend Their Money on: Stuff/Things (basic necessities) nails, clothes, hair, music, televisions, electronics, lotto tickets, scratch-offs, cigarettes, alcohol...etc.

Credit cards, pay-day loans and title loans are making us "SLAVES". Cash is King! Try to pay cash for the things you <u>need</u>. It is so easy to just reach into your purse or wallet and pull out a pretty, colorful credit card and use it for purchases. This is psychological marketing because we know we can pay for it later. When we pay with cash we are more aware of our spending, because the purchase is immediate. In our mind, we aren't losing anything, because when we hand the cashier the card, we get our card back and whatever we brought. When we pay with cash, we visually see the money ($$$) leaving our purse or wallet. There is a feeling of losing something (an even trade). We even feel it! This is where credit card companies make their money, when you do not pay the balance in full before 30 days you are now paying eighteen to twenty-seven percent interest. Maybe, you received a teaser rate for a certain amount of time. Question?????? Did your credit card company inform you that even though you are paying your bill on time, your three credit scores do not go up until your balance is under thirty percent utilization? For example, let's say your credit card limit is $1,000.00 and you charge a purchase of $700.00 for a new TV. Your payment becomes due and you pay the minimum payment of $50.00. So now your balance is $650.00 plus; of course, interest. You still have used sixty-five percent utilization on the card. Your scores do not improve until your balance is under $300 or thirty percent of the original credit limit. Again, pay with cash or just wait and save up for it.

Depreciating Goods	vs	Appreciating Goods
Cars		Real Estate
Clothes		Old Coins
Shoes		Fine Jewelry
Gaming		Metals (Gold, Silver)
Technology		Successful Businesses
Phones		Collectibles (art, fine china)
Nails/Toes/Hair		
Alcohol		

Acre #6 – Setting a Budget for your Family that Works

A budget tells your money where to go. Every dollar should have a name and a place to belong. Creating a budget should be a family affair. Usually it is the children that are continuously asking for "wants". Share the budget with the family. "Train up a child in the way he should go and when he is old, he will not depart from it" Proverbs 22:6 (KJV) Try this free budget program www.everydollar.com

What Three Accounts You Should Have in Your Budget

Account #1 - Emergency Fund (EF) with $1,000 to start and then build up

Account #2 - Savings (can be combined with the EF or separate, but know what they are for)

This money should be in a money market account (keep it liquid)

Account #3 - Retirement Fund- for building wealth (This is for your retirement)

Solid Budget

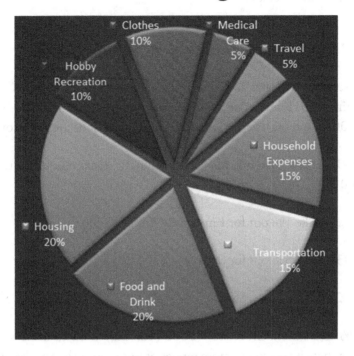

Once you get in the habit of creating and using a budget, it will give you a plan for spending and saving. This should be done in a systematic way. Create this family budget with your spouse or significant other. If you have children, they should also be involved and understand that you cannot buy them everything they want. You, as the parent, must feel comfortable in teaching your children about money and how important it is to stay within the budget. Teach them the difference between "WANTS" and "NEEDS." Keep reading and following this book and I will help you in building financial confidence, so you will feel comfortable about teaching your family members about money. Young children can also learn how to earn an allowance by performing chores around the house or around the neighborhood. The older the child the more they should earn. Now when they want something, have them use their money.

There are generally eight major areas where money is spent during the month. Of course, some areas will require more money than others, since they are a larger expense. The percentages need to equal 100%. To help me to stay on budget, I would place the amount of money allocated for each area in an envelope.

Acre #7 – Steps in Paying Cash with the Envelope Method

I use four envelopes and label them: Restaurants/Groceries, Clothes, Entertainment/Hobbies and Gasoline. Let us look at a household income of $4,000.00 a month (net), after taxes and deductions are taken out.

STEP #1 - Take 10% out for Tithes (church, donations to charities) = $400.00

STEP #2 - Take 5% out for Emergency Fund = $200.00

STEP #3 - Take 5% out for Savings = $200.00

20% Housing = $800

15% Restaurant/Groceries = $600 (You may want to use 2 separate envelopes here if you spend more money at restaurants than at the grocery store)

10% - Household Expenses = $400
10% - Transportation = $400
5% - Clothes = $200
5% - Entertainment/Hobbies = $200
5% - Gasoline = $200
10% - Medical/ Insurance = $400

Take Care of Your four Walls: food, shelter, transportation and basic clothing

"Give not sleep to thine eyes, nor slumber to thine eyelids. Deliver thyself as roe from the hand of the hunter, and as a bird from the hand of the fowler." Proverbs 6:4-5 (KJV)

What is Gazelle Intensity?

In order to understand gazelle intensity, you must know what a gazelle is. A gazelle is any of numerous small to medium graceful and swift African and Asian antelopes. A gazelle is known to be able to run up to speeds of ninety miles per hour for a sustained period, when they are trying to outrun a predator. The gazelle intensity is the running for your life. Run away from your debt as fast and as long as necessary because your life or the life of your loved ones may depend on it.

Notes (Things to remember)

_____

_____

_____

_____

_____

Discussion Questions

1. Have you ever purchased anything on emotions?
2. Have you ever bought something then wished you had not? (buyer's remorse)
3. What does gazelle intensity mean to you?
4. Do you feel that your pre-teen children should be involved in the budget creation?

Activities:

As soon as possible, have a budget meeting with your spouse or significant other to develop a budget and use the envelop system to keep the budgeted amounts of cash in these envelops.

List five ways you can start or continue building your emergency fund.

Go through your home and see what you could sell to add to your emergency fund or pay off some bills. Discuss with your spouse or significant other what you both agree to sell.

Acre #8 – Good News About Debt

This is your next step after building up an emergency fund of at least $1,000. Debt is stealing our wealth from our children and grandchildren. They are watching how you use money, save money, respect money and use credit. Being in debt does not have to last forever. Break the cycle of debt NOW! You can eliminate credit cards, loans and other debt faster than you would expect without using any extra money by "debt snowballing or debt stacking". This method will allow you to pay off debt much faster, but it will take discipline to stay with the plan. Simply list your debts from smallest to the largest amount owed, then pay off the smallest bill as soon as possible. Any extra money you have should go towards this first bill. You want to wipe out this debt. Now take the extra money that was used for the first account and pay it on the second one along with the regular payment. Each time you pay off one account, put the extra money on the next one and watch how quickly your debts go BYE, BYE. Try to pay off as much debt as possible.

Debt Snowball/Stacking ($1,970 per month)

Dillards $20

Zales $80   Zales $100

Visa (3) $220   Visa (3) $220   Visa (3) $320

Stu. Loan $350   Stu. Loan $350   Stu. Loan $350   Stu. Loan $670

Car Loan $400   Car Loan $400   Car Loan $400   Car Loan $400   Car Loan $1070

Mort. $900   Mort. $900   Mort. $900   Mort. $900   Mort. $900   Mort. $1970

Notes (Things to remember)

_____

_____

_____

_____

_____

_____

Discussion Questions:

1. What steps can you take to make sure your credit report is correct?
2. What types of tactics do credit card and pay-day loan companies use to get you to apply for credit or more credit?
3. How do consumers get pressured into using credit for purchases?

Activities:

Arrange all of your debt from smallest to largest and use the debt snowball/debt stacking method to pay-off bills faster

CHAPTER 3

Biblical Plans for our Finances and Giving Back

Key Words

Abundance - Having an overflow.

Generous - Showing readiness to give more of something, as money or time than is expected.

Good Steward - To follow the teaching of Christ, even in finances.

Greed - Wanting much more than you need, focusing solely on oneself and possessions.

Gross Income - Salary before taxes and deductions are taken out.

Myths - Things that are not true, but we believe them to be so.

Net Income - Salary after taxes and deductions are taken out.

Offering - A thing offered either as a gift or contribution.

Servants - Working and helping on behalf of others without complaining.

Stewardship - Working to glorify God.

Surplus - Having extra.

Tithes - One tenth of annual produce or earnings.

Tithing - Giving ten percent to the church for kingdom building or to any organization we believe.

Acre #9 – Have Our Priorities In Order

The Master's Plan (Read Proverbs 13:11, 28:20 (Get rich slow), Proverbs 14:31, 17:5, 21:13 (Give to the poor), Proverbs 6:6-8, Proverbs 13:4, 12:24, 10:4 (Don't be idle) Proverbs 30:8 (Don't be too rich or too poor), Proverbs 23:5, 27:23, Proverbs16:8 (Have your priorities in the right order)

God's plan for our life can be summed up in "Beloved, I wish above all things that thou mayest prosper and be in good health, even as thy soul prospereth." 3 John 1:2 (KJV). Did you notice the key word is prosper? It covers these three areas: your soul, physical health and finances. Poverty, defeat and frustrations are not the will of God. God also shows us how to save for the future. Malachi 3:10 "Bring 10% to God's House"

Psalms 24:1 "The earth is the Lord's and everything in it, the world and all who live in it". God is just and loving, so he is kind enough to allow us to be good stewards with the remaining ninety percent.

Be satisfied and thankful for what God has provided for you. "You must be faithful over a few things, so I will make you ruler over many things". Matthew 25:23

"The borrower is servant to the lender" Proverbs 22:7

Be careful with PRIDE – "One's pride will bring him low, but he who is lowly in spirit will obtain honor"- Proverbs 29:23 (ESV)

P= People
R= Rolling
I = In
D= Debt
E= Eternally

Acre #10 – Why Does A Good Steward Give Back

God wants us to be generous in our giving to others. You can give back in so many different ways to so many different places. Everything I have is a gift from God. I have been blessed beyond measure.

What does it mean to be of good steward?

Being a good steward to me means being thankful with all that has been provided for. Our needs and even some of our wants. God only asks that we take care of the ninety percent that is entrusted to us to manage. Ten percent, actually ALL we have belongs to him, but he allows us to manage ninety percent of it! "No matter how much we give or to whom, our first priority should be to ensure that justice is carried out around us, that we show mercy to our neighbors, and that we practice our faith and not just talk about it. It is through our obedience that Jesus increases our faith". (What Does the Bible Say About….. Nelson 2001). Whether you belong to a church or attend on a regular basis there is work to do around and for our communities. Volunteer your time and energy to a worthy cause of your choosing. One of my ways of giving back is to help others learn about finances and money. The main objective is not to get into debt, but how to build generational wealth for our families.

SPECIAL MESSAGE TO THE PASTORS, PRIESTS, REVERENDS and CHURCH LEADERS

TITHING

How much more would you be able to serve our community if your members were able to give more? What would your offerings look like if your members were financially well-informed?

Financial illiteracy has reached epidemic proportions in our country and causes major problems at both the community and national levels. Eight out of ten people are living paycheck to paycheck which contributes to stress and sleepless nights. This epidemic hurts not only individuals but the community as a whole. The only viable solution to stopping this epidemic is through education.

Many members of our community do not tithe because their spiritual and financial lives are not in balance. In order for a person to have a balanced life, they must be balanced spiritually and financially. Proverbs 21:20 says "The wise man saves for the future but the foolish man spends whatever he gets". Luke 14:28 says "Suppose one of you wants to build a tower. Won't you first sit down and estimate the costs to see if you have enough money to complete it?"

Notes (Things to remember)

_____

_____

_____

_____

_____

_____

Discussion Questions

1. What are some ways you can teach your children or grandchildren about money?
2. How would your ability to tithe change if you were debt-free?

Activities:

If you would like to know all of God's plan for your finances read all of Proverbs. There are 31 chapters. My suggestion is to read one chapter a day for a month. By the way they are short!

CHAPTER 4

Credit Profile

Key Words

1099c - When you settle and pay less to a creditor, they will report it to the IRS and you must add it to your taxable income.

Credit History - The amount of time you have had credit with a company and your payment history.

Credit Utilization - How much of your credit limit you use.

Depreciation vs Appreciation - Value is going down vs value going up.

Inquiries - When you attempt to get credit and the company checks your credit.

Settlements/charge-offs - When you agree with a creditor to pay a lower amount than what is owed.

Acre #11 – Debt is the Wealth Killer

Good Debt	vs.	Bad Debt

Good Debt	Bad Debt
Investment Loans	Credit Cards
Loans for Income	
Producing Real Estate	Personal Loans
Business Loans	Payday Loans
Education Loans	Car Loans

Home Loans

Acre #12 – Know the Differences in Good and Bad Credit

Quick fixes help to dig your hole. (Pay-Day Loans and Title Loans, etc.) Stay away from those places!! Some charge three hundred percent (300%) interest or more interest rates.

What is Credit?

Good Credit:	**Bad Credit:**	**Purchase with Savings:**
Purchases $1000	Purchases $1000	Purchases $1000
Interest Rate 7%	*Interest Rate 27%*	Amount Saved/month $125
Min. Payment $10	Min. Payment $23	8 months to save $1,000
12 years to pay off	12 years to pay off	Interest earned on money in
Interest Paid $440	Interest Paid $2,312	savings $30
Actual Cost $1,440	**Actual Cost $3,312**	**Actual Cost $970**

Activities: Look at how many credit cards you have and what is the interest rate? Can you now cut the card up and call the creditor and cancel the account? Ask them to email you the proof that your account has been closed. You have to make the payments if you still owe a balance.

Acre #13 – What is the Range of Credit Scores?

The Good, The Bad and the Ugly on Credit Scores

- **800-850** **EXCELLENT**
- **750-799** **VERY GOOD**
- **700-749** **GOOD**
- **650-699** **FAIR**
- **600-649** **POOR**
- **300-599** **VERY BAD**

Learn and apply the few steps in repairing your credit quickly.

Having a high credit score really means you have used lots of credit in the past and instead of purchasing items with cash you made those purchases on credit. The smart thing is to change your mindset to using cash for everything when possible, especially for depreciating goods. When you purchase a house, you may need to use credit, but remember it is best to finance for fifteen years instead of thirty years. Your payments will be a little higher, but you will save more money on interest payments. It is wise to even use the debt snowball/debt stacking to pay off your mortgage in less time.

Acre #14 – How to Improve My Credit Scores

Turbo Charge your three (3) Credit Scores
(Experian, Equifax, and TransUnion)

Factors that lower scores	Habits that raise scores
Late payments	On time payments
Multiple Inquiries	Limited Inquiries
Using thirty percent or more of your credit limit	Using less than thirty percent of your credit limit
Applying for lots of new credit	Length of time with the card
Bankruptcies, Tax Lien, or court judgements falls off after 7 years	Homeowner

WHEN 40 ACRES AND A MULE WON'T DO!

Notes (Things to remember)

_____

_____

_____

_____

_____

_____

Discussion Question:

1. What steps can you take to make sure your credit report is correct?
2. What types of tactics do credit card and pay-day loan companies use to get you to apply for credit or more credit?
3. How do consumers get pressured into using credit for purchases?

Activities: Look at your credit card balances. Which ones can you pay down to thirty percent utilization the quickest? Formula: Credit Limit X 30% = amount of 30% utilization

Example: Wal-Mart Credit Limit $1,000 x 30% = $300 Once you have paid this credit card down to thirty percent utilization or under your credit score will go up much faster. The goal is to get ALL your credit balance to under thirty percent (30%) and then down to zero.

Register for www.creditkarma.com to get your credit scores.

CHAPTER 5

How to Buy A Vehicle and Save Thousands

Key Words

Bait and Switch - Advertised low price to get you to the dealership, but that 1 car has been sold.

Closing Cost - These are additional costs added to the price of the car.

Comparison Shopping - Search online or visit other dealerships to see the cost of the same car or vehicle you are looking to purchase.

Convenience Features - These are features on the car that add luxury, ease of comfort or entertainment enjoyment.

GAP Insurance - An additional small cost each month that is included in your payment. This covers the difference in what your vehicle is worth and what you owe if you are in an accident or if your vehicle is stolen.

Lease - Renting the car for a limited period which is usually thirty-six months. Payments are generally lower than purchasing the vehicle. You may also be limited to the number of miles that can be driven on the car.

Options - These may be color choices, interior styles, engine power and wheel designs.

Rebate - Usually at the beginning of the year when the new models come out, the company will offer a rebate or refund a certain amount for buying the newer vehicle.

Safety Features - These are features on the car that add safety (back-up cameras, blind-spot sensors, stop assistance, parking assistance, anti-lock brakes etc.).

Trade-In Value - The value the dealership thinks your car is worth.

Upside Down/Negative Equity - This is the difference of what the dealership thinks your vehicle is worth and what you really owe on it.

Acre #15 – Know How to Negotiate your Next Vehicle Deal

Speaking from experience both as a customer and saleslady, I speak from both sides! This was once my addiction! I like nice, sporty, luxury cars, sporty, luxury and expensive. This depreciating eye-candy had my attention and money for 40 years. I have purchased over twenty-five cars and trucks before the age of fifty-five. What a knuckle-head to buy all of these depreciating goods! Even worst, I was upside down most of the time when I traded in a car. I was caught up in the "No money down" mindset. I would keep a car for two to four years and then something else would catch my eyes.

The Twelve Steps in Buying a Vehicle and Saving Thousands.

1. Know What You Need
2. Know What You Want
3. Do Some Comparison Shopping
4. How Much Can You Really Afford?
5. What to Take To The Dealership?
6. Looking Through the Lot is Exciting
7. The Anticipated Test Drive
8. Your Trade-In (If you Have One)
9. The Discussion between the Manager and the Salesperson

10. Price is Right, Now What?
11. On to the Finance Office (See Step 1)
12. Drive-Out (What are These Gadgets)?

Notice steps one through five should be done before even going to the dealership. Know what you want and need on the vehicle. Every option (bells and whistles) increases the cost of the vehicle. Some options are for added safety: back-up cameras, blind spot mirrors and beepers, sensors, parking and stop assistance, unintended lane changing correction, GPS etc. Also, there are options that are for style, comfort and added individualization like: sport wheels, upgraded stereo system, leather seats, A/C and heated seats, etc.

Take a close look at your budget before buying a vehicle. Will the payments and insurance come to more than fifteen percent (15%) of your household's budget? Is your car payment more than your house payment or rent? Have you checked out the maintenance and repair cost on that particular vehicle? On some vehicles a simple oil change could cost over three hundred dollars ($300). Most luxury cars can only be serviced at the dealership which may cost two or three times more than a good outside mechanic. Insurance is another important expense to research. Each car has a rating and cost. Check to see if the car you want is in demand to be stolen. Thieves target certain cars and trucks.

Can I afford that vehicle?

- What are the costs you will incur when you purchase a car?
- Learn the factors which determines insurance costs on that vehicle.
- Is it best to lease or buy a vehicle? Why or why not?
- Use the Caesar-Time twelve steps to saving thousands of dollars when buying a vehicle.

Always have at least two to four thousand dollars to put down on a vehicle! Why... because you do not want the finance company to roll: tax, title, license, documentation fee, transport fees etc. into the cost of the loan. If you want to trade in a car before it is paid off, you will probably be upside down on the payments (owing more on the car than what the dealer says it is worth). It may be wise to purchase a good used vehicle with cash or lease one instead for three (3) years.

I would suggest getting GAP Insurance while in the finance office. It will pay what you owe on the vehicle, instead of just the value of the car (depreciation) in case the vehicle is totaled in an accident or stolen.

Why Would I Lease a Vehicle?

Lower Monthly Payments

No Negative Equity or Upside Down

Low Maintenance Bills

Lower Down Payments

Stay Up On the Latest Technology

Know the end of lease value upfront (closed end lease)

Certain Vehicles Hold Their Value Longer Than Others

WHAT ARE MY OPTIONS WHEN THE LEASE IS UP?

Refinance and Keep It

Trade It In

Sell It

Turn It In

Frequently Asked Questions

What About the Mileage?

Most car leases last for thirty-six (36) months. Generally, the leasee can drive up to 36,000 miles on the car before they are charged an additional fee per miles. This additional fee usually ranges from $0.10 to $0.25 per mile. Dealerships will generally let you buy extra miles up front, which is less expensive than on the back-end. The up-front cost may be $0.10 extra for 10,000 extra miles which would cost one thousand dollars, but if the extra miles are on the back-end, it would be $0.25, which would cost two thousand, five hundred dollars, which is a big difference!

What About any Damages?

Dealerships expect some wear and tear on the cars after the three years, so a little door ding is expected and generally won't lower the value of the vehicle when the lease is up. On the other hand, if the vehicle has damage from being hit or in an accident, the value will be lowered on the vehicle if not repaired. In my experience, if the ding is no larger than a credit card, it doesn't lose value.

Notes (Things to remember)

_____

_____

_____

_____

_____

_____

Discussion Questions:

1. What add-on features do you think the finance manager will try to add to the cost of leasing a vehicle instead of purchasing one?
2. What do you feel could be an advantage of leasing a vehicle instead of purchasing one?

Activities:

Make a list of three different vehicles that you would like to one day purchase. Write down some features (options) that you must have. Go online and pull up a dealership that sells that vehicle. Compare the prices at a couple of dealerships. Try to do this without leaving your contact information or they just might try and contact you. Try www.truecar.com

CHAPTER 6

Taxes and Allowances

Key Words

Deductions - Are a form of tax incentives, along with exemptions and credits that lowers your tax obligation.

Dependents - The number of children in your home that depend on you financially.

Due Diligence - Doing your own research.

Over Payment - When you overpay your tax obligation and they owe you a refund.

Refund - The difference between taxes paid and taxes owed without interest.

W-2 - An employer must send this form to employees and the IRS at the beginning of the year to report an employee's annual wages and the amount of taxes withheld from their paycheck.

W-4 - (Employee's Withholding Allowance) IRS form for an employee to indicate his or her tax situation to the employer.

Acre #16 – Property Taxes

Taxes, Taxes, and More Taxes

Let's face it! We all have and should pay some taxes. Our first look will be at property taxes. Tax money is needed for the people and services in our communities. Our tax dollars are used to improve infrastructures: bridges, roads, highways, and community services: police departments, fire stations, and health care for many of its citizens. The money also supports school programs. We have a part to play in our communities, but we do not have to overpay our portion. If you feel your property tax valuation is too high, you can dispute the valuation usually up until May. Look around your property at the homes in the front, back and sides of your property. Are they larger, smaller, maintained, junkies etc.? Is your property by a ditch, or bushy area? Are there vacant or abandon homes around you? These properties effect the tax valuation of your property. Be sure to take lots of picture to prove your point. You may be surprised at how much the county tax office may reduce the amount of taxes you owe.

Acre #17 – What about Income Taxes?

Are you happy about getting a tax refund? If you did receive a refund, this means you simply overpaid your tax obligation and received the money back, without interest! Ideally, you do not want to receive a refund or pay taxes after you file your return. There is an effective formula for you being able to give yourself a raise and not overpay your taxes. You should use the extra money in your paycheck for paying off debt and for investment purposes. Be intentional about investments and retirement. More on this thing called "Retirement" later.

Acre #18 – Want a raise, then give yourself one!

Is your W-4 withholdings correct?

Did you know that you can give yourself a raise? This is a 2-part process.

Part 1- <u>Look</u> at the factors below that need to be considered before filling out your W-4. There is a formula for determining how many withholdings you should claim. The higher number of withholdings the **more** money you will have in your check each month. If you are consistently receiving around the same amount every year as a refund, then this could really give your monthly take-home a nice lift.

Part 2 – <u>Invest</u> the additional money you are bringing home. Warning - Do Not Spend It......invest it or even put it in your savings or emergency fund. Remember this is a 2-part process. Just in the event you have to pay some small additional taxes, the money is there. What a great feeling to know you have money saved up!!!!

See formula to determine your allowance in the activity section of this chapter.

GIVE YOURSELF A RAISE
WITH YOUR W-4

Form **W-4**	Employee's Withholding Certificate	OMB No. 1545-0074
Department of the Treasury Internal Revenue Service	► Complete Form W-4 so that your employer can withhold the correct federal income tax from your pay. ► Give Form W-4 to your employer. ► Your withholding is subject to review by the IRS.	20**20**

Step 1:

Enter Personal Information

| (a) First name and middle initial | Last name | (b) Social security number |

Address

| City or town, state, and ZIP code | ► Does your name match the name on your social security card? If not, to ensure you get credit for your earnings, contact SSA at 800-772-1213 or go to www.ssa.gov. |

(c) ☐ Single or Married filing separately
☐ Married filing jointly (or Qualifying widow(er))
☐ Head of household (Check only if you're unmarried and pay more than half the costs of keeping up a home for yourself and a qualifying individual.)

Complete Steps 2–4 ONLY if they apply to you; otherwise, skip to Step 5. See page 2 for more information on each step, who can claim exemption from withholding, when to use the online estimator, and privacy.

Step 2:

Multiple Jobs or Spouse Works

Complete this step if you (1) hold more than one job at a time, or (2) are married filing jointly and your spouse also works. The correct amount of withholding depends on income earned from all of these jobs.

Do **only one** of the following.

(a) Use the estimator at www.irs.gov/W4App for most accurate withholding for this step (and Steps 3–4); or

(b) Use the Multiple Jobs Worksheet on page 3 and enter the result in Step 4(c) below for roughly accurate withholding; or

Acre #19 – Factors to Be Considered When Filling Out Your W-4 Withholdings

- Number of children
- Marriage Status
- Home Ownership
- College/ Retirement
- Number of Dependents
- Employment Status

Example Only:

1 allowance taken	4 allowances taken
$3,000 monthly	$3,000 monthly
- $600 taxes	- $300 taxes
———————	———————
$2,400 take home	$2,700 take home

Take that three hundred dollars and invest it. For the first year, at $300 per month, you have invested $3,600 at 8% interest, you have earned two hundred and eighty-eight dollars. You have given yourself a raise every month and earned interest on your money. This is much better that getting zero percent interest in a tax refund.

- Do you think it is fair that we help pay for government services?
- Do you think the government is best qualified to manage these services?
- Do you think the federal government spends money in a way that aligns with your values?

Acre #20 – Stay Home and Build Your Own Business!

Forget the traffic and having to get up, find clothes, and dress for the weather. Working from the privacy and comfort of home is a great way to earn a living. There are over 3.7 million employees working from home at least half the time. (Source: Funder April 8, 2019) Still one of the best deductions is having a home business. There are many deductions and benefits of working from home and having your own business. Choose one room in your home as an office space. The square footage of the house carries deductions: electric, gas, trash, etc. Any repairs or maintenance you make to the house, if it benefits the office is deductible (i.e., new roof, painting, tree trimming and grass cutting). All supplies and equipment for the business are deductible (i.e., computer, printer, paper, ink, storage and file cabinets, etc.) Let us look at some more business deductions:

vehicle business mileage, vehicle maintenance and repairs. Keep up with your mileage in a mileage record book and keep all receipts (gasoline, maintenance, hotel, food and repairs). Keep personal mileage separate from business mileage. You can either use your receipts or the standard mileage (at the time of writing it was 57.5 cent per mile in 2020) – IRS 2020

Remember: Observe and record the mileage before and after each trip. Also record the mileage on the first day of the year and the last day of the year.

Notes (Things to remember)

_____

_____

_____

_____

_____

_____

Discussion Question:

1. With this information, do you feel getting a tax refund has caused some people to go into serious debt?
2. How could $3,600 in an emergency fund help if your refrigerator broke down or you needed to replace your car's transmission?
3. Knowing you can have large deductions from your home business, what is your passion? What business would you want to start?

Activities: Visit your human resources office and check the number of allowances you are using for your taxes. Are you consistently getting back over five hundred dollars a year on a refund? If so, increase your allowances by one for every five hundred dollars you get back, but please, please remember to invest this extra money!

Example: Refund for 2016 was $1,500/500 = 3
Refund for 2017 was $ 1,600/500 = 3.2
Refund for 2018 was $ 1,550/500 = 3.1

Looking at the numbers above, I would increase my allowance by three. If your financial situation changes, you can go and change your allowances either up or down. If unsure check with your accountant or other tax professional. This is a suggestion, do your due diligence.

What do you think you need to consider before starting a business? We will cover this extensively in chapter 10.

CHAPTER 7

Insurance and Estate Planning

Key Words

Cash Value – Small percentage of growth.

Chronic Illness – Being unable to perform two activities of daily living for at least ninety days (bathing, getting dressed, eating, mobility, continence and toileting).

Critical Illness – Someone having a heart attack, stroke, cancer, organ failure and Alzheimer.

Estate Planning – Important legal forms to have in place in the event of being incapacitated or death occurs.

Living Benefits – The ability to take money out of your policy if you suffer a chronic, critical illness or become terminally ill.

Medical Insurance Bureau (MIB) – Computer database that stores medical and some non-medical information for fraud detection purposes.

Policy Amount - Pay-out amount upon death of an insured person.

Premium - The monthly cost for the insurance.

Risk Factors - Having hobbies or a lifestyle that would put you at a high risk of injury or death.

Term Life – Insured for a certain amount of time (in years).

Terminal Illness – Having a life expectancy of 12 months or less.

Whole Life – Covers you throughout your entire life, but can be very costly.

Acre #21 – Woo-Who.........Let's Talk About Insurance

A study reveals more than forty percent of Americans do not have any form of life insurance. While eighty-four percent of Americans say most people need insurance, only sixty-eight percent say they personally need it and only fifty-nine percent own some form of it. (Source: MarketWatch September 4, 2018) Who must have insurance? **Everyone**, unless you are wealthy. The wealthy can pay for their funeral arrangements and have acquired enough wealth and assets for their families' financial future to continue as before. Most people are not in this category. The purpose of insurance is to transfer the risk of loss from the individual to an insurance company. Insurance is not just for burial, but for the family to be able to continue; with at least, the same lifestyle they enjoyed before the death of their loved one. Insurance should be used to replace the income of the deceased person. Also consider the fact that inflation will happen, so always have enough insurance to cover the foreseen and the unforeseen. Insurance also transfers the risk from yourself to the insurance company. If you do not have any children, debts or assets, then you just need enough insurance for a burial. Always have a will, especially if you have assets.

How Much Insurance Should I Buy? At least six to ten times your annual income. If your annual income is $60,000, you should purchase a $350,000 - $600,000 policy. Of course, if your annual income is $100,000, then you should purchase at least a $600,000 - $1,000,000 policy. Remember, your loved ones will have to live without your income for years to come. Do not forget inflation since the cost of living will increase through the years. If you have a large mortgage and/or lots of debt, you will have to purchase more insurance. Please remember the older you are when you buy the policy, the more the premium will cost per month.

Acre #22 – Compare the Basic Two Types of Life Insurance

Whole Life	**Term** (10, 15, 20, or 30) Years
*More Expensive with less coverage	*Cheaper
*Not an Investment Strategy	*More Coverage
*Builds up cash value slowly	*Ends after the term
*If you borrow against the policy and pass away before it is paid back, that amount is deducted from the face value of the policy	*With the money you are saving you could build up a nice nest egg
*You can't receive the face value and the cash value	

Question: Would you purchase this whole life policy? This is a real example!!

The Monthly Payment is $500.00.

Year	Premium	Cash Value	Benefits
1	$6,000	$314	$950,000
2	$6,000	$1,000	$950,000
3	$6,000	$3,500	$950,000
4	$6,000	$10,000	$950,000
5	$6,000	$25,000	$950,000
6	$6,000	$32,000	$950,000
7	$6,000	$46,000	$950,000
8	$6,000	$30,000	$250,000
9	$6,000	$26,000	$250,000
10	$6,000	$24,000	$250,000
11	$6,000	$23,000	$245,000
12	$6,000	$24,000	$245,000
13	$6,000	$25,000	$245,000
14	$6,000	$27,000	$240,000
15	$6,000	$25,000	$240,000

So…..would you buy this insurance? What happened after year seven? How much premium has been paid by year fifteen? What if, on year fifteen you borrowed the $25,000 from the cash value, then you passed away a month later. How much would your beneficiary really receive? How much premium was paid to receive this amount?

Let's do the math

$240,000 – face value
$25,000 – borrowed
$215,000 – death benefit

$90,000 – premium paid

What does "Buy Term and Invest the Difference" look like?

Example:

Mark and Mary are thirty years old and spend $178 on life insurance each month.

Let's compare the numbers!

Whole Life $250,000	Term Life (20 years) $500,000
* Insurance $178	* Insurance $21
* Investment $ 0	* Investments $157
* At age 50 $34,483	* At age 50 $156,866
* At age 70 $124, 041	* At age 70 $1,865,539
Cash value grows very slowly	* Investment is at 12% interest

If you invest the difference in what you save every month, there will come a time when your investment money has more value than your insurance policy. At that time, you may no longer need life insurance. This is why term insurance is just for a term or for a period of time. You can

44

also (if you choose to) renew the term life until the renewal ends because of age, usually 75-85, you can then purchase a whole life policy. It is costly! Insurance is NOT an investment!

Acre #23 – New Development in Life Insurance, Mortgage Protection, and Final Expenses

In 2016 some insurance companies revolutionized the insurance industry by offering another option to life insurance. One does not have to die to have access to their life insurance money (benefits). Some companies will even allow you to access 100% of your benefits. Why don't we take a closer look!

A new study from academic researchers found that 66.5 percent of all bankruptcies were tied to medical issues-either because of high costs for care or time out of work. An estimated 530,000 families turn to bankruptcy each year because of medical issues and bills the research found. (CNBC 2/11/19)

What Does Mortgage Protection Do for You and Your Family?
Protects Your Family
Protects Your Home Equity
Protects Your Income
Protects and Grows Your Wealth
Protects Your Family from Having to Move After the Death of an Income Earner

You can access the benefits if you have a critical illness, chronic illness or terminal illness and in some cases of an accidental death the face value doubles. It also covers future conditions, and some pre-existing conditions. You do not need a medical exam! There is a four-step process

Application
Prescription History
Field Underwriting
MIB - Medical Information Bureau

Average Funeral cost in 2020 is between $7,000 - $12,000 (lhlic. com). This includes: viewing and burial, embalming, hearse, transfer of remains and service fee. The average cost of a funeral with cremation is $6,000 - $7,000. These costs do not include a cemetery, monument, marker or flowers.

Remember: Your family members are going through a lot of emotions right now with your death. Have everything in order and in a place where at least two people in the family know where to find your important papers and instructions. Your family feels obligated to carry out your final wishes, so have them in writing and do not wait too late. We will talk more about this in estate planning. To see if you qualify for life insurance with living benefits, please contact us at:

Caesarsfinancialgroup.com

Acre #24 – What Other Types of Insurance are Necessary?

Homeowners
Health Insurance
Renters (if you are renting)
Automobile Insurance
Life
Long Term Disability

"Eighty-Four percent of Americans would agree that most people need life insurance, yet when asked, only seventy percent said they needed it." (best life rates 2017)

> ➤ "Forty-One percent of Americans do not carry any life insurance"
> ➤ "Of those who do, nearly one-third have just a basic group policy"
> ➤ "Four in Ten said, "They were under insured and the reminder didn't know either way"

Remember: If you have life insurance through your employer, and you leave the company, you do not have any life insurance. Reason being is that the company owns the policy, not you. Think of it this way! When you go to a restaurant, you are welcome to use the steak sauce, but when you leave, you cannot take it with you. You should have your own personal life insurance.

Other insurance like medical and car insurance carries a deductible which has to be paid first. The carrier pays the difference once the deductible has been paid. A higher deductible will have a lower monthly premium, so a lower deductible will have a higher monthly premium. This is just another reason to have an emergency fund. The larger the better! Strive for at least six to ten times your monthly expenses. Be sure to have an insurance check-up every few years or after major events: birth, death, loss of a job, raise in pay, moving, and college just to name a few. If you decide to change insurance policies, never cancel one until you have received the new policy and it is in full effect.

Acre #25 – Estate Planning is Vital for Everyone

So…. you thought only wealthy people needed to have an estate plan. Think again! If you have a family lawyer, they can help you with the process. Do not procrastinate in completing these forms and then storing them in a safe place. Also make a list of all your belongings and keep this information current.

Important Documents to have in place

❖ **Durable Power of Attorney for Health Care**
A legal document that allows you to appoint an agent to make your health care decisions for you. You must be no longer capable of making your own health care decisions

❖ **Directive to Physicians (Living Will)**
It is a document that allows you to instruct your physician to withhold life-sustaining procedures. Two physicians have certified in writing that the patient has an incurable or irreversible terminal condition and that the application of life-sustaining procedures would serve only to artificially prolong the moment of death.

❖ **Last Will and Testament**

A legal document by which a person expresses their wishes as to how their property is to be distributed at death, and names one or more persons to manage the estate until its final distribution.

Remember: If you have children under the age of 18, it is wise to also have a Guardianship Legal Form in place. This form will designate the person or persons you would like to raise and make decisions on your children's behalf. All of these forms are very important. Let's review the list of forms: Last Will and Testament, Durable Power of Attorney for Health Care, Directive to Physicians (Living Will), Guardianship of Minor Children and a Trust (legal entity that holds property or assets on behalf of another person, group or organization).

Notes (Things to remember)

_____

_____

_____

_____

_____

_____

Discussion Questions:

1. How can one start to have this conversation with their parents?
2. What should you have in place to cover short term disability?
3. Do you feel that renters need to have renter's insurance? Why or why not?

Activities: Check your insurance policy and know what you have. Read the fine print carefully! Some people purchased a policy twenty, even thirty years ago, but do not really know what they have. Even check your parents' policy, since they may have a policy for only $3,000 that was purchased in the 70's or 80's. Remember to check out a policy with "Living Benefits".

CHAPTER 8

Interest and "The Rule of 72"

Key Words

Certificate of Deposit (CD) – Savings account that will receive low interest over time.

Compound Interest – Interest on top of interest

Deposit – Putting money in the bank in some type of account.

Interest- Fees paid to finance something on credit or paid to an investor or individual.

Money Market Account – Savings account that also receives a small amount of interest.

Short-Term Money – Money that you want to use in a short period of time like six months to one year.

Withdrawal – Taking money out of the bank from an account.

Acre #26 – Knowing this Rule can Make or Break You

How long will it take for YOUR money to DOUBLE?

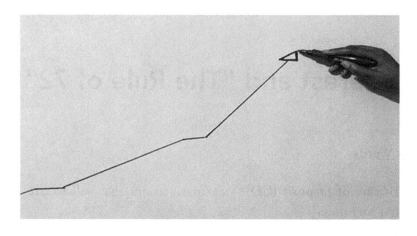

What is This "Rule of 72" or "Banker's Rule" and why is it so important?

This simple, but effective rule is generally not discussed too much in your local banks. If you understood this rule......well, you might have second thoughts about the low, low interest rate you might earn. Remember your emergency fund and short-term money should be in a savings account and not your long term/retirement money. Check out the numbers on this scenario.

You walk into a bank to deposit $2,500, and you see on the marque that the rate for return on deposits today are as follows:

- CDs one year **up** to 1.0 % APY ($500 to open)
- Money Market Accounts 1.17% ($2,500 to open)
- Saving **up** to 1.20 APY ($10,000 to open)

Looks like since you have $2,500, you will be opening a money market account and accruing a 1.17% interest rate

The rule of 72 or banker's rule is this..... Whatever the interest rate, divide it into 72, and that is how many years (at that rate) it will take for your money to double.

For Example

2% interest = 2 divided into 72 = 36 years for your $10,000 to grow to $20,000

6% interest = 6 divided into 72 = 12 years for your $10,000 to grow to $20,000

12% interest = 12 divided into 72 = 6 years for your $10,000 to grow to $20,000

As you can clearly see the interest rate determines your rate of wealth. Also know "Time is Money". The earlier you start investing, the better!

This rule works against you when you are paying interest but works the same way. If you are paying interest on something still divide the interest rate into 72 to see how quickly what YOU OWE will double.

Example: 24% interest on a $2,000 purchase (24/72 = 3 years what you owe will double until you have paid it off). This is compound interest in a bad way because it goes against the consumer.

Notes (Things to remember)

_____

_____

_____

_____

_____

_____

Activities: Go into any bank or drive down the highway and check the signs that have an advertisement for the bank. At the time of this writing the average interest paid on a deposit will earn 2.50% interest. At this rate it will take almost 25 years for your money to double.

I AIN'T GOT TIME FOR THIS!!!!

Keep researching to find out where to find 6 % - 25% on your money. Powerful, because 72 divided by 25% is only 3 years for your money to double. By the way, you do not have to start with $5,000 to invest.

Remember: Interest can either make you or break you! If you are earning interest that is a GOOD thing, but if you are paying interest that is a BAD thing.

Notes (Things to remember)

_____

_____

_____

_____

_____

_____

Discussion Question:

1. What does this rule mean to consumers?
2. How can this rule make or break your wealth?
3. Do you think bankers and credit card companies should explain this rule to all their customers? why or why not?

Activities: Look online to see which financial institutions offer the highest rates on both money market accounts and CDs. What is the minimum amount that has to be deposited and for how long to get that rate of return?

CHAPTER 9

Making Student Loans Affordable

Key Words

Deferment- Temporarily stops or reduces federal student loans, based on some type of hardship.

FAFSA – A Free Application for Federal Student Aid.

Forbearance- This may be an option if someone is struggling to make payments.

Forgiveness Programs - Can cancel all or a portion of an individual's Federal Direct Loan Payment. This may be the case with public service jobs and teachers. Some districts may offer this as an incentive to come and teach in their schools.

Grants- Money for college that does not need to be paid back.

Refinancing- May lower the amount paid overtime usually through private lenders like banks and credit unions.

Scholarship- Money that is awarded to deserving students that meet certain qualifications.

Acre #27 – Be Smart About College Cost

In 2018 Americans owed more than 1.4392 trillion in student loan debt (studentloanhero.com Feb. 4, 2019). The average family owes over $45,000 in student loan debt. Parents need to help their children make the choice on which college or university to attend. Remember only 54.8% of college students graduate in six years. (Abigail Hess cnbc.com Oct. 10, 2017). Many students are racking up over $45,000 in debt without anything to show for it, meaning they did not graduate! Not only that some students may decide to change their major before finishing their degree. Have a plan and stick with it. It may be a good idea for your student to attend a community college to get their basics out of the way. This by itself will save you thousands of dollars. Many students get a part-time job while going to school and stay at home with their parents for at least two years. Advanced placement (AP) classes in high school help to prepare students for the rigor and difficulty of college level classes. AP classes also assist students in being offered scholarships. The number one reason thirty percent of students drop out of college in their first year is due to a lack of discipline and the second reason is finances.

Tuition Price Averages

Private (four year) college: $32,000/ a year
Public (four year) out-of-state college: $24,000 a year
Public (four year) in-state college: $9,500 a year
Public (two year) community college: $3,500 a year

Having a well-funded emergency fund could take care of college cost without getting loans. Fill out the FAFSA to apply for Free Federal Aid for college. Make sure to apply for all scholarships and grants that may be available and ones that your student qualify for. There are all types of scholarships through: organizations, churches, academics, and athletes. They may range from a few hundred dollars to thousands of dollars. Millions of dollars in scholarships go unclaimed each year because they were not applied for.

Notes (Things to remember)

_____

_____

_____

_____

_____

_____

<u>What About Forgiveness Programs?</u>

Forgiveness Programs: Public Service Loan Forgiveness (PSLF) Program can cancel some or all of an individual's Federal Direct Loan Balance (public service jobs and teachers).

Qualifications

One has to be in the program for up to 5 years
If you miss a payment, you will be out of the program
This is a government program and can be
stopped or changed at any time

Acre #28 – Never Stop Learning

No HS Diploma
$493 Weekly
$25,636 Annual

HS Diploma
$678 Weekly
$35,256 Annual

Master's Degree
$1,341 Weekly
$69,732 Annual

Associate's Degree
$798 Weekly
$41,496 Annual

Bachelor's Degree
$1,137 Weekly
$59,124 Annual

Notes (Things to remember)

_____

_____

_____

_____

_____

_____

Discussion Questions:

1. Look at your student's G.P.A. (Grade Point Average) Is it at least a 3.0 in high school?
2. How many AP classes has the student attempted and passed?

Activities:

Start looking early for colleges to attend. This conversation should start while the child is in middle school.

Get all paperwork done in a timely manner.

Require your student to visit their counselor every week to check on scholarship information at the beginning of their senior year.

CHAPTER 10

Retirement Plan and Business Savvy

Key Words

Age/Global Trends/Balance Consideration

Due Diligence – To do your own research.

Financial Gap – The financial difference of where you are and where you would like to be.

Life expectancy – How long a person can expect to live.

Risks- Probability of losing something.

Social Security – An amount that the government will pay to individual after they reach a certain age.

Acre #29 – What to Consider Before Retiring?

* Do I/We have three to six months of income in my/our emergency fund?
* Are we debt free, except for the mortgage?
* Where you want to live?
* Risk Tolerance/Age?
* Your health?
* Due Diligence of the Investment Firm (research)

What is Dollar Cost Averaging?

Dollar cost averaging is investing a set amount each month into your investment account, like a mutual fund. Regardless if the value of your fund goes up or down, you are consistently investing the same amount. When the value or price of your stocks (fund) goes down, then the price of a share is cheaper, so you can accrue more shares. This is considered a SALE! When the share prices climb or go back up, you have more shares than if the price had never gone down. Cool! Check out this example:

* Invest $100 every month to buy shares
* Price per share is $20, so I get 5 shares
* The market price went down to $10 a share
* Now I can buy 10 shares, instead of only 5
* When the price goes back up or increase, I now have more shares (value)
* This is considered a SALE (Bargain)

I LOVE THIS STUFF!!!!!

Notes (Things to remember)

_____

_____

_____

_____

_____

_____

Most People Will Work: 40 years or more

40 hours a week or more

Then retire with 40% of their prior income

What will their life generally look like at age 65?

100 people age 65

Forty-Five percent depend on family/friends

Thirty percent depend on social security or charity

Twenty-Three percent still working

Two percent self-sustaining

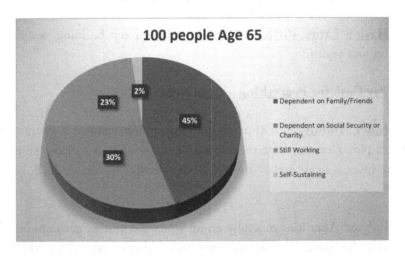

Most people are outliving their money. This does not have to be your story or your children's story. Your financial education could literally transpire into your following generations being financially free or even wealthy.

We need to quit talking about retirement planning and start talking about planning for when you can no longer work. Retirement was not intended to last 30 or 40 years.

One out of every three males and one out of every two females who are currently in their mid-50s will live to be 90 years old.

Acre #30 – Retirement is not an Age but a Financial Number!

Be Ready for Inflation – Be intentional about retirement. Retirement is not an age it is a financial number. Invest, Invest, Invest

Continue Investing in Stocks - The potential return from stocks over time is more likely to outpace inflation when compared to cash or banks according to Wells Fargo report.

Put-Off Collecting Social Security - You can claim at 62, but if you wait until 70 your monthly check could be twice as much.

Have a Large 401(k), 403(b), or IRA - Keep building wealth all throughout your life

Pay Cash for Everything – Cash is King

Index Annuity – A type of investment that features a guaranteed return plus a market base return, with less risk than a variable annuity. Some investors call it the "Best of Both Worlds" (Investopedia July 28, 2019).

Indexed Annuities generally go up when the market goes up, but do not ride the market down. Nice way to build generational wealth! This could be a good way to finance a college education for your children or grandchildren. Think about this….What if you placed $5,000 in an index annuity and let it ride the market up for 18 years when Baby John Doe was graduating from high school. There could be $50,000 or even $60,000 in the account. Nice start for college!

Acre #31 – You Want to Start Your Own Business and be Your Own Boss?

I believe there is a business in all of us. You just have to know your passion and follow the process for making it successful. Having a hobby is a whole lot different than having a business, so do not treat your business like a hobby or you will make hobby money. Let's get started!

#1-Know your Why?
#2 Know Your Niche (Who)
#3 Identify Your How
#4 Develop an Effective 15 second Elevator Pitch

When someone ask, "What do you do?" How will you answer that question?

Example: I help individuals and families get out of debt and build wealth for now and in the future, by assisting them to fill in the gaps of where they are now and where they want to be.

Notes (Things to remember)

_____

_____

_____

_____

_____

_____

Activities: Write an elevator speech for your potential business. This is a living and breathing document, so change it as needed and practice your pitch until you have it down smoothly.

"STEPS TO YOUR OWN SUCCESSFUL BUSINESS"

- 1. Your Passion/ Knowledge
- 2. Investment Budget?
- 3. A Partner?
- 4. What Aspects Would You Rather NOT Do?
- 5. Start From Scratch or Purchase an Existing One?
- 6. Home-Based Business
- 7. Employees? Licenses?
- 8. Business Models/Franchising?
- 9. Who Can Assist You in Learning?
- 10. Create a Business Plan, Research

    Liability, Register Your Business
- Finally.....Don't treat your business like a hobby, if you want to make BIG $$$$

Notes (Things to remember)

_____

_____

_____

_____

_____

_____

Acre #32 – The Important Business Plan

BUSINESS PLAN
Format

Executive Summary

(Who is the business?)

Vision Statement
(How are you prepared to provide the service
outlined in the executive summary)

Mission Statement
(Why did you choose this particular business?)

Culture
(What core values are you prepared to instill in your business?)

Business and Industry Profile
(What industry and how has it changed? Will the
industry support your business long term?)

Company Description
(How will the business be broken down? Who
will own it? What's the target market?)

Structure-
Target Market-
Goals Include-

1.

2.

3.

4.

5.

Business Strategy

(Why should consumers use your business?
What are you attempting to achieve?)

SWOT Analysis

Strengths-
Weaknesses-
Opportunity-
Threats-

Competitive Strategy
(What gives your business the edge to succeed?)

Company Services
(What particular services are you providing?)

Customer Benefits
(How will the customer benefit from your company?)

Marketing Strategy and Plan
(How do you plan on marketing your business:
price, product, place and promotion?)

Product(s)/Service(s)
(How will you price the products, services provided?)

Pricing
(What will your products and services cost?)

Promotion
(How will you promote your business?)

Location
(What are the advantages/disadvantages of the location?)

COMPETITIVE ANALYSIS

The competitive analysis is a statement of the business strategy and how it relates to the competition. The purpose of the competitive analysis is to determine the strengths and weaknesses of the competitors within my market, strategies that will provide me with a distinct advantage, the barriers that can be developed in order to prevent competition from entering my market, and any weaknesses that can be exploited within the product development cycle.

COMPETITIVE POSITION
FIVE FORCES MODEL OF COMPETITION

The five forces of competition model are used to provide a better understanding of your business industry. These five forces include: the threat of new entrants, the bargaining power of suppling, the bargaining power of buyers, the threat of substitute products, and rivalry among competing firms.

1. The threat of new entrants -
2. The bargaining power of suppling -
3. The bargaining power of buyers -
4. The threat of substitute products -
5. The rivalry among competing firms -

PERSONNEL PLAN

The Personnel Plan reflects the objective of providing an ample amount of service personnel.

FINANCIAL FORECAST

Cost of starting the business: Incorporation, salary, insurance, licenses and permits. Also, the cost of stationary, communications and the creation of a digital footprint.

FUNDING REQUEST and EXIT STRATEGY

How will I get my money and what happens if the business does not succeed? What is my exit strategy?)

Notes (Things to remember)

_____

_____

_____

_____

_____

_____

Discussion Questions:

1. Why is it a good idea to know your market?
2. Who do you know that can mentor you in your quest for a business?
3. What kinds of business do you think would be profitable in the next 2-3 years?

Activities:

Think of one or two businesses you would like to start in the next year, if the money was there?

What would you do to market your business now and in the future?

Let us practice writing another elevator pitch or use the first one and really make it flow and be you.

CHAPTER 11

Investing 101

Key Words

Compound Interest – When your money continues to double depending on the interest rate.

Consolidated- To bring together into a single or unified whole.

Diversify – Having the right mix of stocks, bonds and other investments.

Dow Jones Industrial Average- DOW, a financial publishing firm in New York City, showing the average closing prices of the common stocks of 30 industrials, 20 transportation companies, or 15 utilities.

Foreclosure- The act of foreclosing a mortgage or pledge.

Liquidity – Having quick and easy access to your money.

Market Correction – Decline of at least ten percent or more in the market (generally last days to months or longer) This can be scary in the short term, but a correction can be a good thing, adjusting overvalued asset prices and providing buying opportunities.

Stock Market- A particular market where stocks and bonds are traded; stock exchange.

Volatility- Stock exchange value when it is likely to change suddenly.

Acre #33 – Risks and Growth in Balance

The markets have been riding smooth with low volatility for a few years now, but on August 14, 2019 volatility jumped back into the stock market marking the 4th largest drop in history with an 800.49 point drop or 3.5% by the Dow Jones Industrial Average. (CNBC) In the next 3 days it was up again three percent. From time to time the market will have a correction. We will discuss later about what to do and how to prepare for the ups and downs in the market. What we do know is this – more people are buying homes since foreclosures are down, but the prices of homes and rentals are going up also, less people were buying vehicles which could weigh on the United States economy. Automakers may have to reduce jobs if sales continue to decline. Some banks are closing their doors or consolidating their services. In 2017, the number of banks that closed were eight, none closed in 2018, and four closed by November 2019. Some closed to save money because less people were making deposits with smaller amounts. Simply, some Americans started finding a better place to keep their funds, and maybe even received a decent return greater than two percent interest. You can't build wealth if that is what you are trying to do with these low returns, but banks do have a purpose depending on your financial goals. You will not build wealth in a savings account, but your money is liquid, which means you can have access to it right away.

Acre #34 – Compound Interest Builds Wealth

Da BOMB DIGGITY!!
COMPOUND INTEREST

- Making money from money
- Did you know if you start saving and investing a $100 a month before you are 21, you have a good chance of having over a million dollars by age 65?

Different Kinds of Retirement Funds and How They Work

401(k)- A 401(k) is a retirement savings plan sponsored by an employer. It lets workers save and invest a piece of their paycheck before taxes are taken out. Taxes are not paid until the money is withdrawn from the account.

403(b) – Is a retirement savings plan sponsored by an employer for public education organizations, some non-profit employers, cooperative hospital service organization, and self-employed ministers in the U.S.

Solo 401(k)- Is a qualified retirement plan for Americans that was designed specifically for employers with no full-time employees other than the business owner(s) and their spouse(s).

Roth IRA – Is a special retirement account where you pay taxes on money going into your account and then all future withdrawals are tax free. This is best when you feel that your taxes will be HIGHER in RETIREMENT than they are right now. In 2019 the income limit is $122,000. For singles it will increase to $124,000 in 2020. For married couples filing jointly the max is $193,000 but will increase to $196,000 in 2020. The maximum a person can contribute if age 49 or under is $6,000. A person who is 50 and older may contribute a maximum of $7,000 in 2019. www.investopedia.com

Simple/Tradition IRA- Allows an individual to get a tax deduction for money that is set aside for retirement. The contributions and earnings are NOT taxed until they are withdrawn. Under some circumstances you may get a partial withdrawal from your account.

SEP- IRA – A Simplified Employee Pension IRA is a variation of the IRA. It is adopted by business owners to provide retirement benefits for themselves and their employees. The contributions cannot exceed $56,000 and are subject to annual cost-of-living adjustments for later years. (www. irs.gov).

Compound Interest Builds Generational Wealth

Activity: If you had an opportunity to trade a penny for $1,000,000 dollars, yes $1,000,000 or wait for it to compound interest (double) for 31 days, which one would you prefer? You may want to use a calculator for this one. The first 7 days are done for you. See diagram below! If you choose not to write in your book, take a piece of paper and number down the side from 1 – 31. The answer will be on the next page, but I know you can do the math and figure it out for yourself. Don't forget to place your decimals in the right spots!

Day 1 $.01	Day 2 $.02	Day 3 $.04	Day 4 $.08	Day 5 $.16	Day 6 $.32	Day 7 $.64
Day 8	Day 9	Day 10	Day 11	Day 12	Day 13	Day 14
Day 15	Day 16	Day 17	Day 18	Day 19	Day 20	Day 21
Day 22	Day 23	Day 24	Day 25	Day 26	Day 27	Day 28
Day 29	Day 30	Day 31				

$10,737,418.24

Not sure where to find this rate of return. Let me know if you do! You see how compound interest works. Let us try a more realistic rate of return. What would an eight percent return look like on a $10,000 one-time investment into a mutual fund?

Year 0	$ 10,000
Year 9	$ 20,000
Year 18	$ 40,000
Year 27	$ 80,000
Year 36	$ 160,000
Year 45	$ 320,000
Year 54	$ 640,000
Year 63	$1,280,000

THERE ARE THREE PURPOSES FOR INVESTMENTS: PROTECT, EARN AND GROW

Protect: To keep what you have save. Your priority is safety and not earning interest or growth. This may only keep up with inflation.

Examples: savings accounts, CDs, money market accounts and U.S. Treasury bills

Earn: Giving up a little control. Giving money to a company who will promise a regular, predictable income that may out perform the rate of inflation.

Examples: utility stocks, fixed income mutual funds, corporate and municipal bonds

Grow: Investments that generally appreciate in value. Can be risky if the company doesn't show any or much capital growth.

Examples: stocks, growth stocks and real estate

What is diversification? Have you ever heard the term having all your eggs in one basket? In investing, you want to have a good mix depending on your goals and what you are trying to accomplish. The goal of diversification is to reduce risk and to protect yourself against losing money.

Notes (Things to remember)

_____

_____

_____

_____

_____

_____

Discussion Questions:

1. What are your goals for investing?
2. If you must have a credit card go onto www.creditkarma.com to check out the interest on their credit cards.

Activities:

How much interest is your savings account or CDs receiving now and figure out how long it will take for your money to double using the "Rule of 72".

CHAPTER 12

Investments in Real Estate

Key Word

Acquisition – The act of receiving something (real estate).

Compound Interest – When your money continues to double depending on the interest rate.

Dollar Cost Averaging – Consistently depositing the same amount of money each month.

Equity – In terms of equity in a home, it is the difference between what you owe on your home and what it is worth.

Exit Strategies – Getting rid of something, usually through selling.

Hard Money Lenders – individuals that have money usually in a retirement account that they will lend on real estate for a short amount of time until a loan is acquired (generally up to five years).

Hybrid – Combination of tax deeds and tax liens, but the property owners may buy back their properties during the redemption period set by state statutes and pay the back taxes plus interest.

Passive Income – Income that is made that isn't connected to a job.

Redemption Period – A period of time to receive something back.

Sectors – Category of different types of investment and how they are grouped together.

Tax Deed – Tax delinquent properties are sold for back taxes owed.

Tax Liens – Is a lien imposed by law upon a property to secure the payment of taxes.

Acre #35 – There are Only a Few Things You Can Do With Money

(Spend It, Save It, Invest It, Give It Away, Hide It)

FINDING THAT MONEY CAN BE FUN

- Pay off credit cards, Never buy things you don't understand, Have a garage sale
- Consider raising your deductibles on car(s) and home(s), Use FREE entertainment
- Cancel your PMI=Private Mortgage Insurance, if you have built up twenty percent equity in your home
- Use COUPONS & DOUBLE COUPONS, Shop with a list, Switch cable service
- Limit eating out, Does your car really need premium gasoline
- DON'T PLAY THE LOTTO OR ONLY BUY 1 TICKET, Refinance your home, Watch those extended warranties
- Forget name-brand clothes/shoes, Buy generic, it may have the same quality
- Do your own hair (go natural), nails, toes and car wash, purchase a car that is two-three years old
- Do not spend money on the latest and greatest electronics

Acre #36 – Ways to Create Wealth in Real Estate

Renting vs Buying...Why is Real Estate Such a Good Investment?

1. Appreciate in Value
2. Depreciation for tax savings (itemization)
3. Equity builds up throughout the loan
4. Leverage is increased return on investment (ROI)
5. Residual/Passive Income

Formula for (ROI) Return on Investment

Income Property Evaluation – Capitalization Rate Formula Cap Rate

Example

Property Price (total investment)	$150,000
Number of units	1
Property Address 54321 Mary Doe Drive	
Monthly Rent	$ 1,600

(If you have a property management company let them set the rent for the area)

Gross Income (rent X 12 months)	$ 19,200
Operating Costs (1-4 units = 30%, 4+ units = 40% gross rent)	$ 5,760

(maintenance, insurance, taxes, vacancies, property management etc)

Net Operating Income (NOI) = Profit at the end of the year	$ 13,440

NOI / Property Price (total investment) X 100 = Cap rate%

$13,440 / $150,000 = .0896 X 100 = 8.96

A good cap rate usually falls between 4 – 12%. Also look at actual rents and expenses.

Acre #37 – Which Type of Real Estate Deals are Best for You?

Foreclosures - Short-term, quick cash, and you will need to bring some cash to the table

Lease Option – Appreciation and cash flow (rental)

Mobile Homes - Cheaper investment, cash flow (rental)

Rehabbing - Cash flow, quick cash, need cash

Tax Deeds or Foreclosure Sales - May attain properties cheap

Wholesale buying and contract sales - Low cash required, and quick cash

Acre #38 – Example of a Buy and Hold Deal

RENTAL PROPERTY DEAL

THE "SWEET DEAL" WITH HARD-MONEY LENDERS FOR INVESTMENT PROPERTIES

Used mainly for delinquent mortgages, foreclosures, and bankruptcies

Cost of House	$50,000		
Repairs	$10,000	PROS:	Fast investment capital, can't obtain a conventional loan, backed by the value of the property and not credit score,
Total	$60,000		private individuals or corporations, simple and fast closings in 1 to 10 days
Down Payment	$ 5,000		
Balance	$55,000	CONS:	Lower loan-to-value (LTV) ratio, (riskier to the lenders) often ranging from 60-75% of the total property value, term 12 months or less, interest rate 12-21%, points added to loan (usually 3-6 pts)

Acre #39 – Make a Whopping 25 – 50% Interest in Texas

TEXAS PROPERTY TAX SALES-TAX LIEN CERTIFICATES AND TAX DEEDS

www.tedthomas.com

Pay property taxes that the county need for: parks, building schools, roads, libraries, fire stations, etc.

Redemption period is six months to two years (homestead or agricultural property).

Twenty-five percent (25%) INTEREST – 1st year.

Fifty percent (50%) INTEREST – 2nd year.

Tax Lien Sale gives you the right to collect the past due taxes, plus interest.

You can foreclose and own it.

Know the rules for your county.

Look up public notice website (Texas Legal Notice) tax auctions for the month in the state and property addresses.

FINDING AUCTIONS

Each county has rules and regulations that must be followed

(Bexar County Tax Collector Albert Uresti's Website)

Investigating Properties: size, neighborhood, **condition** (see for yourself, take pictures, google and www.zillow.com) and **minimum bid** (phone call or internet search)

Acre #40 – "The Big Ideas"

1. Your mindset can either make or break your budget. Stay focused and have discipline!
2. Have a budget and stick with it. This is a family affair!
3. Be thankful for what you have and be a good steward.
4. If you cannot pay cash then wait until you have the money. Cash is King!
5. Be in control of your car deal. Know exactly what you want and need. Always purchase GAP insurance.
6. Do not overpay your taxes and give yourself a raise by knowing how many allowances to claim.
7. Be sure to have the correct kind and amount of life insurance. Remember with Living Benefits, you do not have to pass away to be able to use your money.
8. Know and be able to calculate the "Rule of 72". This can make or break your finances!

9. Attending a community college is much cheaper than a university. If you have a strong student that has passed several AP classes in high school, they may be able to handle the rigor of college courses. This takes discipline!

10. Be intentional about your finances. Retirement is not an age, but a financial number. Be ready!

11. Compound interest builds wealth! Research and do your own "Due Diligence" when investing. Know what your expectations are for investing.

12. Real estate is still one of the best, if not the best ways to invest and grow your wealth.

CHAPTER 13

The Mule

Hopefully, **"When 40 Acres and a Mules Won't Do"** has given you and your loved ones a host of helpful strategies and tips to understanding how money really works. We get pulled from all directions about how and what to spend our money on. It is time we push and pull towards our own financial success. Please share this book and the strategies with others that you care about. Tell others about the advantages of having a solid financial plan in place. Our country needs to open up the conversation about money. "Closed Mouths Don't Get Fed". Eighty percent of Americans are living paycheck to paycheck. My prayer is that these numbers decrease as quickly as possible. It only takes one missed paycheck or an illness to crush a family's saving and retirement fund. Be prepared for the unexpected! Build that emergency fund to take care of at least four to five months of expenses. Put at least ten to fifteen percent of your paycheck into a retirement account and stick with a budget each month.

We are in control of our finances, so be intentional about your financial future and success. To contact us for more information, please visit our website: caesarsfinancialgroup.com

KNOWLEDGE IS POWER, BUT APPLICATION IS SUCCESS!

Be Blessed!

Printed in the United States
by Baker & Taylor Publisher Services

Printed in the United States
by Baker & Taylor Publisher Services